In the fold...

In the fold...

Life's
most
essential
folding
techniques

Stewart, Tabori & Chang · New York

Designed by Larissa Nowicki
Edited by Marisa Bulzone
Graphic Production by Kim Tyner

Published in 2004 by
Stewart, Tabori & Chang
115 West 18th Street
New York, NY 10011

Canadian Distribution:
Canadian Manda Group
One Atlantic Avenue, Suite 105
Toronto, Ontario M6K 3E7
Canada

Library of Congress Cataloging-in-Publication Data

Robinson, D.J. (Dawn Jackson)
    In the fold / D.J. Robinson ; illustrations by Harry Bates.
        p. cm. – (Finishing touches series)
        ISBN 1-58479-381-3
        1. Napkin folding. 2. Paper work. 3. Textile crafts. I. Title. II. Series.

TX879.R68 2004
642'.79–dc22

                                                        2004003965

Printed in China by C&C Offset Ltd.

10 9 8 7 6 5 4 3 2 1

First Printing

Stewart, Tabori & Chang is a subsidiary of LA MARTINIÈRE
GROUPE

To my mother, Ada Jackson, and the memory of my father, Jesse Jackson Jr., who has gone on to be with the Lord and is already in the fold.

Thanks to everyone who helped me get this book researched, written, and published. Adrienne Ingrum, my friend and prayer partner, who hired me to write it. Toni Barton and her assistant Tera White for spending all day patiently photographing the folds for illustrator Harry Bates; designer Larissa Nowicki; editors Marisa Bulzone and Trudi Bartow and copyeditor Ana Deboo; cousin Clarice Taylor-Bell for suggestions and resources; friends Geoffrey Johnson and Lana Turner for last-minute supplies (like Lana's shoe bags–things I would never think of owning!); Damian Sanchez for tips on folding clothes; Cashawn at Macy's for tips on wrapping gifts; and Mrs. Puthie Cadwell for tips on packing.

My friends at work, some of whom are still wondering how I got this gig: Shirley Wong, Delores Thompson, Roberto "Sarge" Sanchez Jr., Sunny Lee, Dennis Pittman, Rosemary Black, and Anthony Conners for their various tips.

My husband, LaMarr Robinson, who asked why it is every time I take up a project, he always ends up doing a lot of the work, and son Isaac, who did a little modeling without protest, and who both allowed me the time away from home to complete the book. Special thanks to the New York Public Library, and to all my friends and relatives who kept me in prayer through my Lord and Saviour Christ Jesus.

Introduction

Working with your hands brings fulfillment and a sense of accomplishment. Using traditional home arts in their purely practical applications simplifies our complex lives. This little book teaches basic techniques of folding, one of the most essential home arts, not in the abstract, but practically, for today's busy lives. Yet it also presents the beauty of folding, honoring the simple traditions from which these methods are drawn and preserving them for the future.

As expected, *In the fold...* will show you how to fold napkins into impressive table decorations and great holders for flatware, saucers, rolls, and even fruit. But napkins are only the beginning. Mothers who are environmentally conscious or have babies who are allergic to disposables will appreciate the section on folding diapers. Everyone will value the instructions on how to fold clothes and linens so they don't have to be ironed again after they are taken out of drawers and closets (as well as the tips on organizing storage spaces to accommodate these time-saving folds). *In the fold...* also offers stylish options for folding handkerchiefs for suit jackets and the traditional technique for folding the American flag.

A section on packing and a chapter on folding party hats and favors ensure that *In the fold...* has something for everyone.

We all give gifts, and **_In the fold..._** puts an end to cookie-cutter, store-assembled gift packaging, with visual instructions for elegantly folded wrappings that are as special and personal as the gifts beneath the folds. A final project introduces the ancient Asian art of origami.

Napkins: Folds That Hold

When I was a little girl, we used to play a game called **Four Corners**. We first folded a piece of notebook paper and carefully tore off the top to make a square. Next, we folded the corners to make four triangle shapes, then turned the sheet over and folded four more triangle shapes at the corners. Finally, we folded the whole thing in half so there were four pockets for our index fingers and thumbs on both hands. We wrote numbers on the outside of the pockets, colors inside each pocket, and scrawled an embarrassing question or funny message on the inner portion of the folded game.

Years later, I learned an impressive napkin configuration that is folded the same way as that old origami game. It is called the **Place Mat Fold**, because you can place a saucer or plate in the center of this large folded napkin. Once you have mastered this fold, it will not embarrass you. In fact, it's quite versatile. A few more folds produce the **Artichoke Fold**; a pull or two more and you have the **Water Lily and Rose Fold**. You can place fruit or a dinner roll in the center of each. The **Buffet or Pocket Fold**, which is very easy to fold but looks complicated, holds the fork, knife, and spoon.

> Before folding any napkins, make sure the napkins, your hands, and the surface on which you will be folding are spotless and clean. Iron all napkins before you start and, for perfect creases that hold, iron each fold as you go along.

> If napkins are made with a hem stitch, place them with the front side facing upward, toward you, as you begin the folding steps.

> Napkin fabrics vary from linen to cotton to linen-and-cotton blends to synthetics. I prefer cotton because linen can be too expensive (to me) for folks to wipe their hands on. The synthetics don't hold the folds as well cotton. But everyone has their preference. Some starch their napkins, but I would rather steam iron. There are ways to get stains out, but sometimes you just might not want to interrupt dinner to whisk a napkin into the kitchen for immediate stain treatment.

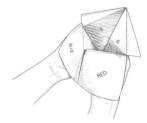

"Pick a number," we'd say. Then we counted while our index fingers and thumbs maneuvered the doohickey. "Now pick a color." .

1

Place Mat Fold

1. Position the napkin in front of you diagonally and fold the corners to the center. Each of the four folds will be the shape of a triangle.

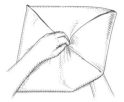

2. Gently gather the center to keep the folds in place as you turn it over on the opposite side.

3. Fold the corners to the center again as you did on the opposite side. Again, you have four triangle shapes.
4. Hold the folds in place again and turn the napkin over.

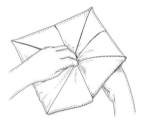

5. Take the tip of each fold from the center and fold it back to its outer corner. Then place your saucer or plate in the center.

2

Artichoke Fold

1. Position the napkin in front of you diagonally and fold the corners of the napkin to the center. Each of the four folds will be the shape of a triangle.

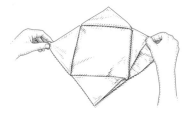

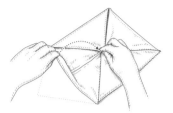

2. Repeat the same step by folding the new corners into the center.

3. Gently hold the folds in place and turn the napkin over.

4. Fold the corners once into the center as you did on the opposite side.

5. Place your fingers in the center and gently pull out and up on the corners from the opposite side, forming the buds. Place a dinner roll or fruit in the center.

Water Lily and Rose Fold

1. Follow each step of the Artichoke Fold (see page 14). In addition, pull out the flaps from the opposite sides that are between the folds that you pulled out and upward.

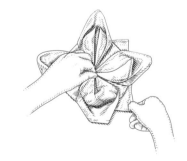

2. Pull the folds (buds/petals) up a little more for the Rose
   Fold. Place a dinner roll or fruit in the center.

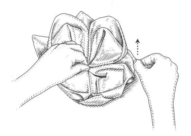

4

Buffet or Pocket Fold

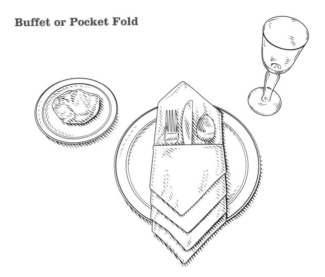

1. Fold the napkin in half into a rectangle.

2. Fold in half again into a square.

3. Position the napkin so that the top right corner has the four loose edges.

4. Fold the top flap down to the front of the bottom edge. The fold is shaped like a triangle.

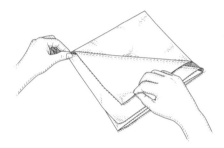

5. Fold the next layer down but not as far as the first fold so that it has a layered look.

6. Fold the third layer down and as before, again not as far as the previous fold.

7. Fold the right and left sides backward about an inch. For larger napkins, fold the sides backward about 2 inches.

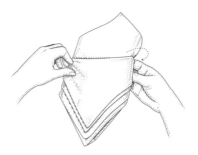

8. Tuck your utensils underneath the third layer.

Informal Table Setting

1. Plate in the center.

2. Saucer on top of plate.

3. Knife to the right of plate.

4. Spoon to the right of knife.

5. Dinner fork to the left of plate.

6. Salad fork to the left of dinner fork.

7. Glass to the right in front of knife and spoon.

8. Napkin to the left of salad fork or on top of saucer—unless the napkin is holding utensils, in which case place it and all utensils to the right of the plate.

Folding Clothes and Linen

> *O bed! O bed! delicious bed!*
> *That heaven upon earth to the weary head!*
>
> THOMAS HOOD, *HER DREAM*

A few years ago, my husband and I ordered a four-piece wardrobe unit that took us seven nights to assemble. We had to work on the project after our son, who was an infant at the time, went to sleep because otherwise he picked up pieces and crawled away with them. It was hard enough to put it together with all the parts right there in front of us!

Once we finally completed it, we threw all our clothes on the shelves and closed the doors. It looked nice from the outside, but inside our shirts, blouses, sweaters, pants, and skirts looked like big wads of crumpled paper, and we had to iron everything before we could wear it. Learning to fold and then disciplining myself changed that.

Folding clothes the right way used to be part of life. Now it's an art form. I asked several dry cleaners how to fold a shirt properly, but most shrugged their shoulders. "We send our stuff out," they said. The exception was Damian Sanchez, a young man who works at a Midtown Cleaners on Manhattan's West Side and who used to work at a place where the neighborhood cleaners sent their "stuff" to be folded.

When it came to folding fitted sheets, I should have sent them out because what I was doing was more fumbling than folding. But there is a way to fold fitted sheets so they look just as neat as folded flat sheets.

My husband is a restless sleeper who wakes up sleeping directly on the mattress due to what I call the "jerky foot." Now I put straps on the fitted sheet and mattress pad to keep them in place, and by making mitered, or hospital corners, I can ensure that the top sheet also stays in place.

1

Shirts, Sweaters, Blouses, and Why <u>Not</u> to Fold Pleated Skirts

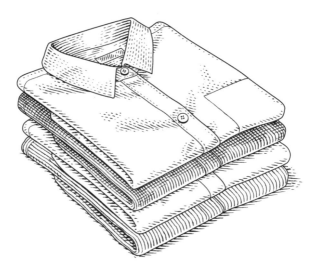

1. Find a clean surface large enough to lay the shirt flat.
2. Button the top three and bottom two buttons on a man's shirt and all the buttons on blouses.

3. Lay the front of the shirt facedown.

4. Pull both sleeves out to the sides and smooth.
5. Make sure the collar is in place. If folding a turtleneck, fold down the collar.
6. Take the right sleeve and fold it over to the left sleeve, folding the right shoulder one-third over where the collar begins.

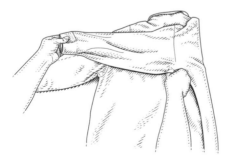

7. Take the right sleeve and fold it back over the right side at the armpit.

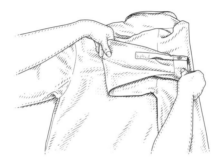

8. Fold the sleeve from the edge where the shirt is folded back over to the left like a fan.

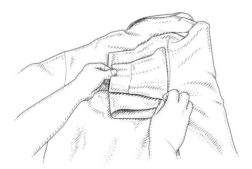

9. Take the cuff and fold it back to the left.
10. Repeat the same steps with the left sleeve, going toward the right.

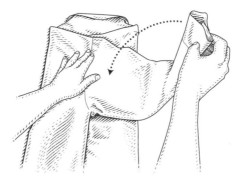

11. Fold the shirt into thirds. Fold the bottom of the shirt up about a hand's length.
    Fold it again to meet the edge of the left sleeve and again to the back of the collar. Turn it over.

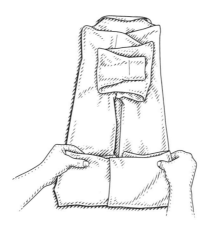

🖝 Use the same steps for blouses and women's sweaters as folding a shirt, but take note that designers often expand women's collars, so you can't always use that as a guideline for folding into thirds.

🖝 Some things should not be folded, and the pleated skirt is one of them. Otherwise, it would have to be ironed every time you wanted to wear it. Store your pleated skirts on multiskirt hangers. When ironing a pleated skirt, peg it with clothespins at the bottom of the pleats first. To pack it, store it in a garment bag or, if you are not carrying a garment bag, lay the skirt flat before you place it in the suitcase and safety pin the pleats at the bottom. Place the skirt inside a dry-cleaner's plastic bag.

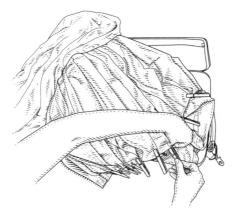

2

Quick and Easy Asian Fold
for Shirts and Sweaters

My friend and co-worker Shirley Wong was sent an e-mail
from Taiwan with step-by-step instructions for folding clothes
in half the time it takes the traditional way.

1. Lay the shirt or sweater flat, front upward.
2. With your right hand, take hold of the right side of the shoulder's top edge about an inch from the collar.

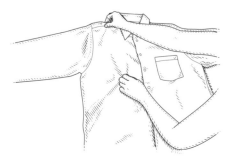

3. Grab front and back layers with your left hand straight down from the position where you have your right hand on the shoulder, and straight across from the armpit.

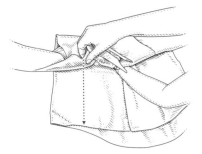

4. With your right hand still holding the shoulder's edge, bring it over the left hand to the bottom edge of the shirt. The edge in your right hand should be parallel to the bottom edge.

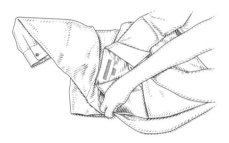

5. Using the left hand, pull the shirt out toward you. If there are long sleeves, shake a little to allow them to fall through.

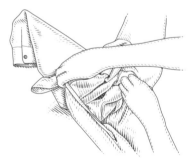

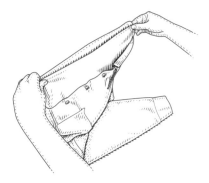

6.   Lay the shirt facedown and fold the sleeves and back over the center of the shirt.

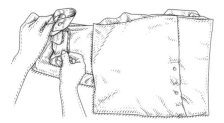

7.   Turn it over to the front. A perfect fold.

3

Folding Fitted Sheets

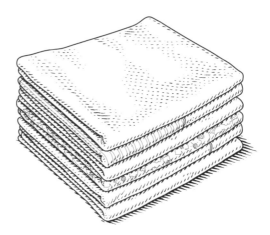

1. Place your left index finger into the outside of one corner.

2. Take hold of a parallel corner with your right hand and tuck the left corner into the inside of the right corner.

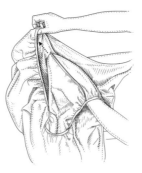

3. Fold and smooth the creases so that the elastic edges are folded down and there is a straight fold across the top and the right side making an L shape.

4. Repeat the same step on the other end.

5. Fold the four edges in a square or rectangle.

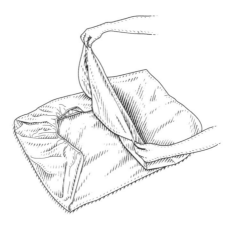

4

Making a Bed with "Hospital" (Mitered) Corners

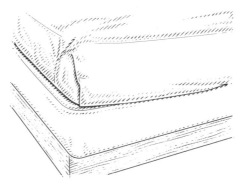

1. Lay the sheet on the bed, aligning the top edge of the sheet with the top edge of the mattress.

2. Tuck in the sheet at the foot of the bed.

3. Pick up the side edge of the sheet about 15 inches from the foot of the bed.

4. Make a diagonal fold onto the bed. It should look like a triangle.

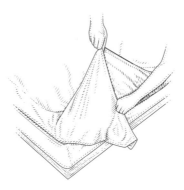

5. Tuck the part of the sheet that is hanging over the side under the mattress.

6. Pull the diagonal fold on the bed down and tuck it under the mattress.

Organizing Storage Space for Folded Items

The hardest part of organizing storage space is keeping it that way. Staying organized is an ongoing task.

- Store folded shirts, blouses, sweaters, pants, and skirts by seasons and category: dress shirts, T-shirts, thick sweaters, and so on. The best time to start organizing is at the change of a new season, because you accomplish two purposes: bringing your seasonal clothing out and folding last season's clothes neatly.

- If you have the space, keep guest linen separate from your everyday sheets. Place scented tea bags or sachets among the linens to keep them from smelling musty.

- If you have the space, keep the linen in the room where it will be used. I keep my son's linen in his room, our linen in our room, and tablecloths, napkins, and kitchen towels in a drawer in the kitchen.

- To keep everything organized and folded, YOU have to do it. There's usually one—and only one—in each household who cares enough about organization to make the effort. You can teach your children to fold and store, then pray that they take heed. The best time is when you do the laundry. Get them to help out. (Notice I didn't say teach your spouse. This is not a lesson on wasting time.)

- Put all the clothes you need to give away in boxes or bags. Put in the things you are going to wear again when you lose weight and items you are hoping will come back in style. Unless you are one of those people who wears only vintage clothing, give out-of-date clothing to someone who will appreciate it. Make a separate bag for things no one would want to wear. It goes to the garbage or gets transformed into rags.

- Put clothes that are in constant use on easy-to-reach shelves. When removing folded clothes to wear, lift clothes from the top gently, then place them back neatly, so that everything stays in order.

☛ *Cedar drawers are excellent for repelling moths, but they aren't effective if you go in and out of them every day. So only use cedar drawers for your long-term storage.*

Packing Efficiently

My main objectives in packing are to carry on my baggage and not iron what I've packed. I have a roller case that fits snugly in overhead compartments. My husband has a bag that he carries over his shoulder, and our son's clothes go in his backpack. If we need dress clothes, we put them in a garment bag that folds and can also be carried on board.

- When choosing what to pack, color coordinate to mix and match outfits. One blouse could go with slacks as well as a skirt.

• Put a pair of dress shoes in a plastic bag, and wear the casual shoes. Lay slacks and jeans, folded just once, along the length of the suitcase. If you are not taking a garment bag, lay skirts and dresses the same way. Fold shirts and sweaters as shown previously. Jackets can be folded the same way as shirts, if not put in a garment bag. Then wrap them in tissue paper or plastic dry cleaning bags before arranging them on top of the slacks and dresses. Place the bagged shoes in the bottom corner. You are ready to go!

☞ *Mrs. Puthie Cadwell from Arizona, who has been packing and repacking for many years, recommends rolling up the underwear and placing them inside the folds of the larger items to prevent hard creases.*

Miscellaneous Folds

What do a diaper, handkerchief, flag, and book cover have in common? Nothing, you might say, except that they are all things that are folded. But they're all also attached to something or someone: a diaper goes on a baby's behind, a handkerchief goes in a suit pocket, the flag goes up a pole (although not when it is folded), and a book cover goes on a book. So all of the folds in this section are miscellaneous "attachments" to one thing or another.

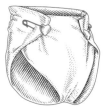

When my son was born, I decided to use cloth diapers because I prefer natural things. I went and bought a dozen of them—but I only lasted about a week as this all-natural mother before I exchanged the bag of unopened diapers for a bag of disposables.

My husband made fun, reminding me that I had vowed that "no disposables are going on my baby's behind." I wasn't as natural as I thought I was, but I still admire those who stick with cloth diapers. So, for mothers who choose cloth diapers because they are environmentally conscious or whose children are allergic to disposables, here is how to diaper a baby.

Also included is how to fold handkerchiefs, for men who like to add a little style to their suits. My husband calls this fold the Double Dutch. It is an easy, not too fancy fold that adds a nice touch.

According to a recent poll, 55 percent of Americans are more patriotic today than they were 25 years ago, and more than 60 percent own an American flag. Included here are instructions for the proper folding of the Stars and Stripes.

Have you ever read a book that was a bit too risqué for public display? Or do you just want to protect the covers? (Once I was taking a course at my church where we had to read several books. But one book's title was a little too personal for my taste, so I covered it with a book cover as I read it riding the subway on my way to work.) These are instructions on how to make your own paper book cover, whatever your reason for wanting one.

1

Diapering a Baby

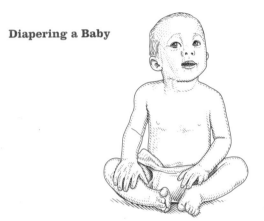

1. Lay the diaper flat and fold the sides across to meet in the center.

2. Fold a third of the bottom diaper to the front.

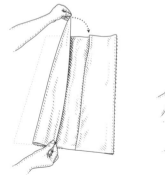

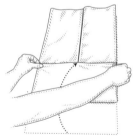

3. Unfold the top center edges out diagonally.

4. Place the baby on the diaper and bring the front of the diaper up between the baby's legs (just under the healing navel, if the baby is a newborn).

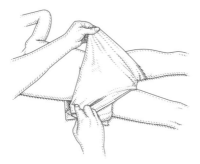

5.	Bring the flared edges from the back to the front and fasten with pins or clips.

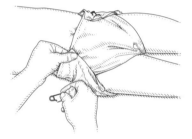

☞	*For double absorbency, use two diapers and fold the top diaper several times lengthwise to make padding. Then continue as instructed above.*

2

Double-Dutch Handkerchief Fold

1. Lay the handkerchief out flat diagonally.
2. Fold it in half to make a triangle.

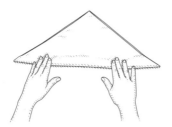

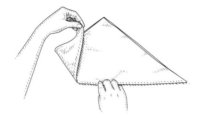

3.   Fold both sides into the center, creating a diamond shape.

4.   Fold in half from bottom up creating another triangle.

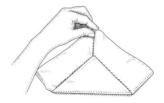

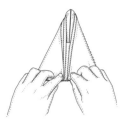

5. Fold both sides into the center, creating a smaller diamond shape.

6. Tuck into pocket with two loose ends facing front and top.

3

The United States Flag Fold

The tradition is to raise the United States flag at daybreak, then lower it and fold it at dusk.

1. Fold the flag in half lengthwise.
2. Fold it again lengthwise, with the striped section covered by the blue field.

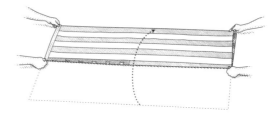

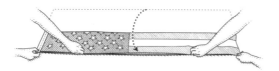

3. Starting at the striped end, make a triangular fold, bringing the folded edge up to the open edge.

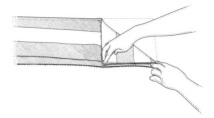

4. Fold the pointed end inward to make another triangular fold.

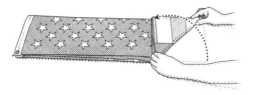

5. Continue in this way until only one fold remains. At this point, only the blue field will be showing.
6. Fold the last flap of the flag into a triangle and tuck it into the already-folded portion to secure the bundle.

4

Paper Book Cover

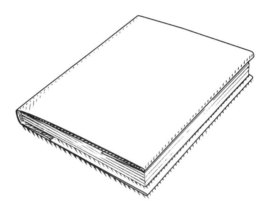

1. Make sure you have enough paper to cover all sides of your book. Lay the folded but not creased paper on a table and place the book on top with its spine about an inch or more (depending on the book's thickness) from the fold.

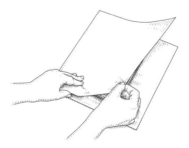

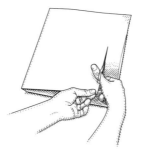

2. Cut the paper out around the book, leaving about an inch on all three sides. (Do not cut the folded edge.)

3. Crease and fold in the top and bottom edges. It should be the same length as the book.

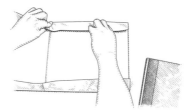

4. Place the book inside the folded paper.

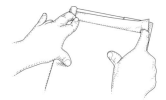

5. Fold and crease the paper into the opening right side of the front cover.

6. Turn over and fold and crease the paper into the opening left side of the back cover.

☛ *The flaps of the cover also work as bookmarks. And you can use any type of paper you like, including the brown paper grocery sacks.*

Fancy Paper Folds

One of our neighbors, Rose, left a gift for our son outside our door. Wrapped in orange and green scarf fabric and gathered at the top, it looked like a colorful flower vase. Attached to the gathered string was an Easter bunny.

"What is it?" my husband asked.

"It's one of Rose's decorative creations. You know she's an artist." I took off the bunny and gave it to our son and set the vase on the TV set.

The next time that I ran into Rose, I thanked her for the gift. She asked if our son enjoyed the chocolate.

I looked at her, dumbfounded. Chocolate? She explained the chocolate was inside the wrapping. I had to confess that I thought the wrapping was the gift.

Later, I took the chocolate (partially melted from sitting on a warm TV) out of the "vase." Some gifts are almost too beautiful to unwrap!

This section will also include instructions on folding party crowns and favors for a child's party and an origami project using a dollar bill from a book by origamist John Montroll.

1

Wrapping Boxed Gifts

1. Place the wrapping paper on the table with the box in the center. Overlap the paper to make sure there is enough to cover the box.

2. Cut the wrapping paper to size. You should be able to completely encircle the box top to bottom and left to right, with an additional $1/2$-inch overlap.

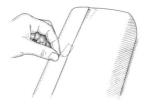

3. Place the box upside down on the wrapping paper with the top and bottom centered and close enough to the left side to fold over about an inch on top. Fold the left side over the box, crease it, and fasten it to the box with tape.

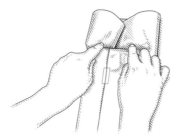

4. Fold the extended paper at the right of the box so that it overlaps the taped portion, crease it, then turn the edge under $\frac{1}{2}$ inch and tape it.

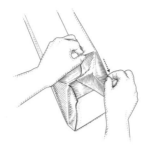

5. Fold the bottom open edge over the box and crease it.

6. Crease both triangle sides that have formed and fold the triangle sides toward the box.

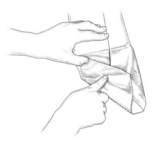

7. Fold the flap that is formed up over the box, turn in the edge, and tape it.

8. Repeat steps 5 through 7 for the top end of the box.

2

Wrapping Oversized and Complicated Gifts

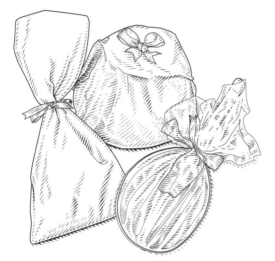

1. Place the gift in the center of the wrapping paper and cover it
    loosely to ensure correct size. Set the gift aside.

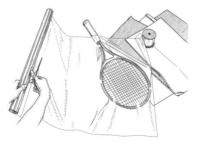

2. Cut about a hand's length of extra paper for the fringe or ruffle at the top. Set this paper aside, along with the string—cut to about an arm's length—you are going to use.

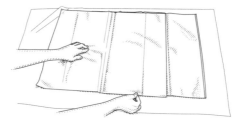

3. Place tissue paper inside the wrapping paper.
4. Place the gift in the center of the tissue paper and gently smooth both layers of paper upward around the gift, regardless of its shape.

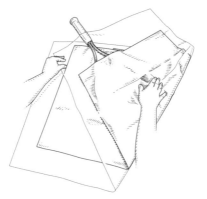

5. At the neck of the gift, gather all the sides and use the string to secure the wrapping in place.

6. Arrange the loose edges of the paper at the top.

➤ *If you need to wrap something that sticks out, like a tennis racket, roll the handle in the same paper and secure it with tape. Then wrap the bottom as instructed above, leaving the handle poking out of the gathered paper.*

☞ Cashawn, who wraps gifts at Macy's department store in New York City, said it took him about four months to get it just right. He says that the trick to wrapping an extra-large box is to wrap half the box first, then wrap the other half, making sure the paper overlaps the first wrapping. Place the ribbon so that it covers the overlapped edge around the entire box.

☞ There is a noticeable difference between expensive and inexpensive wrapping paper, but using the latter isn't always inappropriate. Think about who your gift is for—a child who will quickly tear through the paper to get to the gift or an aesthetically inclined friend who will savor beautiful paper and unwrap the package with loving care?—and choose accordingly.

3

Party Crowns

Make sure the napkin or construction paper you use is at least 20 inches square, or your crown will look more like a party beanie.

1. Fold a paper napkin or a piece of construction paper in half diagonally.
2. Fold the long edge up 1 inch, then repeat this twice.

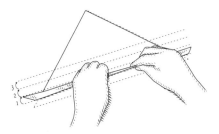

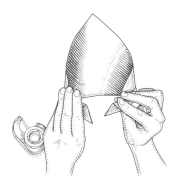

3. Turn the hat over.

4. Fasten the two long ends with tape, glue, or staples.

5. Decorate the front by gluing on colorful pieces of cut paper and other ornaments.

☞ *To make your hats into animal faces, complete steps 1 and 2, but fold the band only twice. Turn the paper over and fold the right side over the left and the left side over the right, then staple the two sides. Turn the paper over and draw your animal's face.*

4

Paper Airplane

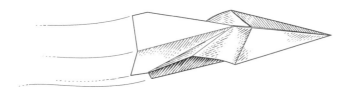

1. Fold an $8\frac{1}{2}$-by-11 inch sheet of plain paper lengthwise in half, crease it, then unfold it.
2. Fold the top right corner in to the center and crease the top.
3. Repeat with the left side.

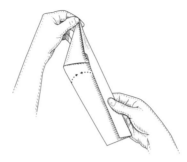

4. Fold the paper lengthwise in half again. The flaps should be on the inside. It looks like a rocket.

5. Fold the top right slanted edge into the center and crease the edge all the way back.

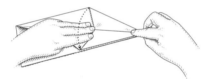

6. Repeat with the left side. It still looks like a rocket.

7. Crease back the right wing edge starting about 2 inches down from the top point.

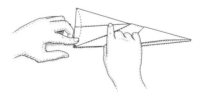

8. Repeat with the left wing.

5

Origami Swan

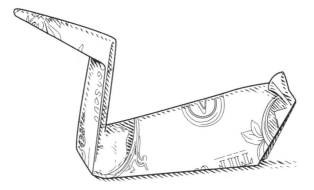

1. Fold a dollar bill in half lengthwise. Crease it and then unfold it.

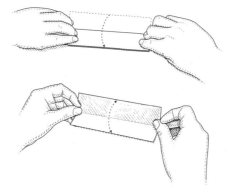

2.	Fold all four corners diagonally to the center.

3.	Fold the two corners of one end diagonally to the center again.

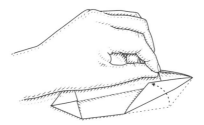

4.	Fold the same side again. It should look like a teepee.

5. Turn the bill over and fold the back toward the front with two points meeting.

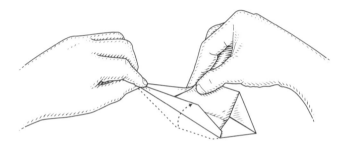

6. Take the front folded-over tip and fold it about half an inch.

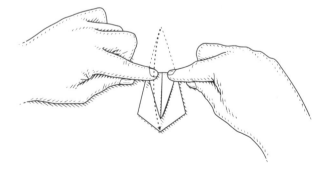

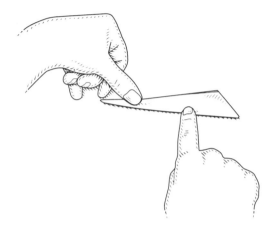

7. Fold in half lengthwise.
8. Pull up the top to form the neck and head.

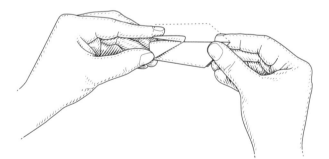

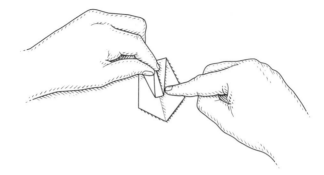

9. Tuck in the tail and pull it up.

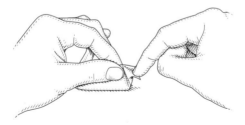

Bibliography and Resources

If you want something done right, you have to do it yourself.

MY MOTHER, AND PROBABLY YOURS TOO

The Art of Gift Wrapping
Alexandra Eames and Carol Spier, Smithmark Publishers Inc.,
New York

Diaper Changes, the Complete Diapering Book and Resource Guide
Theresa Rodrigues Farrisi, M. Evans and Company, Inc., New York
1997

Napkin Folding
James Ginders, Three Rivers Press, New York, 1978

The Simple Art of Napkin Folding
Linda Hetzer, Hearst Books, New York, 1980

The Art of Napkin Folding
Bridget Jones and Madeleine Berhaut, Anness Publishing Inc.,
New York, 1994

Dollar Bill Origami
John Montroll, Dover Publications, Inc., New York, 2003

America's Housekeeping Book
New York Herald Tribune Home Institute, Charles Scribner's Sons, New York, 1941

Useful Websites

Dy-Dee Diaper Service www.dy-dee.com

United States Flag and Flagpole Store www.united-states-flag.com

House & Garden Television www.hgtv.com

Martha Stewart Living www.marthastewart.com

Oprah www.oprah.com

Real Simple magazine www.realsimple.com

Dawn Jackson-Robinson's interest in home arts and crafts is the result of heredity and necessity. After moving into her pre-war co-op in Harlem fifteen years ago, where she now lives with her husband LaMarr and son Isaac, she began several ongoing restoration projects. When her parents drove from Kentucky to New York to deliver a new sleigh bed that her father made, they proceeded to sand and varnish her wood floors, make curtains, replace light fixtures, install a new sink and basin, and tile the kitchen—all in a week's visit!

She admits that she and her husband are not as quick and skilled in their work as her folks were, but their projects range from stripping woodwork of layers of paint dating back to 1916 to upholstering antique and used furniture. Most of their projects are still "in progress." The two small closets that provide all the built-in storage space in their apartment have made folding a necessary skill.

When she is not writing poetry—or working on one of her home projects, or folding for pleasure, or practical reasons—she is a researcher at the *New York Daily News*, where she has worked for twenty years. Born and reared in Georgetown, Kentucky, she received her B.A. in Broadcast-Journalism at Western Kentucky University, and her M.A. in Creative Writing at the City College of New York. She is a member of Bethel Gospel Assembly in Harlem.